MEDITERRANEAN DIET
SIMPLE DIET GUIDE WITH DELICIOUS RECIPES FOR RAPID WEIGHT LOSS

© **Copyright 2015**

All rights Reserved. No part of this book may be reproduced in any form without permission in writing from the author. Reviewers may quote brief passages in reviews.

Disclaimer

No part of this publication may be reproduced or transmitted in any form or by any means, mechanical or electronic, including photocopying or recording, or by any information storage and retrieval system, or transmitted by email without permission in writing from the publisher.

While all attempts have been made to verify the information provided in this publication, neither the author nor the publisher assumes any responsibility for errors, omissions or contrary interpretations of the subject matter herein.

This book is for entertainment purposes only. The views expressed are those of the author alone, and should not be taken as expert instruction or commands. The reader is responsible for his or her own actions.

Adherence to all applicable laws and regulations, including international, federal, state and local laws governing professional licensing, business practices, advertising and all other aspects of doing business in the US, Canada, UK or any other jurisdiction is the sole responsibility of the purchaser or reader.

Neither the author nor the publisher assumes any responsibility or liability whatsoever on the behalf of the purchaser or reader of these materials. Any perceived slight of any individual or organization is purely unintentional.

Contents

INTRODUCTION...5

CHAPTER 1: ALL ABOUT THE MEDITERRANEAN DIET 7

CHAPTER 2: THE BENEFITS OF THE MEDITERRANEAN DIET................................14

CHAPTER 3 THE MEDITERRANEAN DIET – SOME FUNDAMENTALS 18

CHAPTER 4: GETTING STARTED................... 33

CHAPTER 5 RECIPES................................... 42
- Breakfast 42
- Lunch 53
- Dinner 66
- Dessert... 80

CONCLUSION..89

Introduction

I want to thank you and commend you for reading the book, "Mediterranean Diet: Simple Diet Guide with Delicious Recipes for Rapid Weight Loss"

The world holds as many diets as there are food types. Fad diet after fad diet comes out causing a stampede of people headed for the gym or the supermarket for the next best ingredient. They all have one goal – healthy wellbeing and weight loss.

Why should the Mediterranean diet be any different?

Because it does not place many restrictions on its followers. Instead, it encourages the enjoyment of life. Most fad diets promise fast results, whereas the Mediterranean diet promises longevity and a richer life without the assistance of supplements or pills.

Throughout this book, I will give you an introduction to the Mediterranean diet, some basic information and a handful of recipes to get you started.

By the end of the book, I hope you'll find the Mediterranean diet appealing and easy to integrate into your lifestyle. As with everything, healthy living means healthy choices. I hope to encourage you toward healthy choices or confirm your current healthy lifestyle while giving you fresh inspiration for your meals.

Throughout this book, I have added several hyperlinks whereby you can continue reading on the given topic. These hyperlinks are also used to credit the information I have written.

I trust that you will find this book informative and inspiring. Living a healthy lifestyle helps each of us to experience life to the fullest. Life is meant to be lived, enjoyed, and experienced.

Chapter 1: All About the Mediterranean Diet

Let's take eating back to its natural fundamentals – clean, fresh eating. With supermarkets and grocery stores stocking up on processed foods or foods laden with preservatives and chemicals, we need to take ownership of our eating habits and intentionally pursue a healthy, active lifestyle. In this chapter, I am going to expand on the Mediterranean diet and where it came from.

What is the Mediterranean diet?

The Mediterranean diet is a goodness-packed diet of fresh fruits and vegetables, whole grains, olive oil, fish, poultry, and red wine. This diet is the natural lifestyle of countries along the Mediterranean Sea, specifically Southern Italy and Greece.

Since these countries are located near the Mediterranean Sea, they have many nutritional advantages regarding fresh produce year-round, as well as a constant supply of fish and seafood, all of which are packed with omega-3s and other essential fats.

The Mediterranean Diet avoids added sugar, refined grains, processed food, trans fat, and refined oil. Even with these no-go foods, people can experience many pleasures on this diet including physical activity, social gatherings, and celebrating life.

The Mediterranean diet focuses on a variety of foods throughout the year to vary the sources of nutrients your body receives. In contrast to the Western diet, the Mediterranean diet reduces salt intake to a minimum, substituting herbs for excessive salt.

Looking at the history of the Mediterranean diet

The countries along the Mediterranean Sea make up the Mediterranean Basin, the central hub of society during ancient times. The exact origins of the Mediterranean diet have been lost in history; however, we do see the influences of three main cultures, namely Roman, Germania, and Arabic.

The Roman culture followed the Greeks in consuming bread, wine, and oil. The Roman aristocrats consumed fish, seafood, fresh produce, and sheep cheese; in contrast, the lower class Romans ate mainly bread, olives, and olive oil.

The Germanic view of food focused on beer, home-grown vegetables, and domestic pigs.

These two lifestyles clashed and partially merged before meeting the Arabic world. The Arabs introduced other plant-based foods such as pomegranates, citrus, rice, eggplants, etc.

Thus the Mediterranean diet began to evolve over the years. The discovery of America further enhanced the diet with the addition of potatoes, corn, tomatoes, and chili.

Where did the cereal aspect of the diet originate? Due to the cost of more nutritious foods, the poorer people and slaves would be given cereals as a way of keeping their hunger satisfied for longer.

Fast forward to the 1950s where we meet American scientist Ansel Keys, who was the first to draw a correlation between cardiovascular disease and diet. He wondered why poorer populations in South Italy were healthier than New York's upper classes.

The result was the *Seven Countries Study* held in Finland, Holland, Italy, US, Greece, Japan, and Yugoslavia. This studied concluded that those on the Mediterranean diet had a lower rate of cholesterol and minimal heart disease than those on the Western diet.

The Lyon Diet heart study and another study published in 2008 in the British Medical Journal confirm a reduction in the risk of cardiovascular disease, cancer, Parkinson's, and Alzheimer's.

We can safely conclude that adopting the Mediterranean diet into your lifestyle will go a long way in improving your chances of longevity.

The Mediterranean diet pyramid

With the Mediterranean diet, you don't have to stress over counting calories. Of course, as with every diet you can count calories if you want to, however, emphasis is placed more on food proportions than calorie count.

The Mediterranean diet pyramid was created in 1993 by *Oldways Preservation and Exchange Trust, the Harvard School of Public Health* and the *World Health Organization*. The pyramid is on the next page:

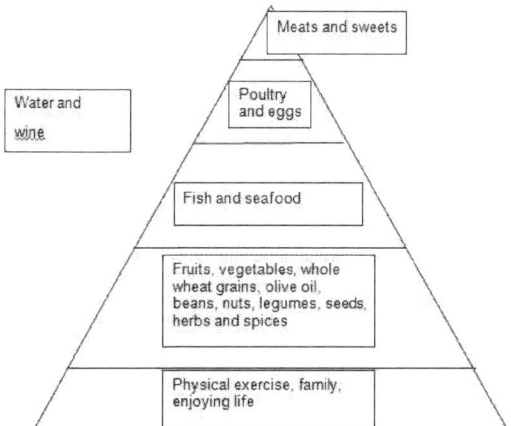

The Mediterranean diet follows the above pyramid by focusing on three meals a day. These three meals consist of the following:

- One to two servings of cereals per meal. Types of cereals include bread, pasta, rice, and couscous. Focusing on whole grains will ensure that your body is getting essential nutrients, including magnesium and phosphorus.

- One to two servings of vegetables at lunch and dinner. Ideally one of these servings should be raw. By eating vegetables with two of your three meals you are allowing your body to absorb a variety of antioxidants.

- One to two servings of fruits at all three meals, including dessert. Try to avoid other desserts as much as possible while turning fruit into a delicious fresh dessert.

- Two or more servings of fish and shellfish during a week. Eggs can be consumed up to four times a week, whereas red meat is limited to two servings per week.

- Legumes and potatoes are more than two servings per week.

- Dairy products are consumed in the form of low fat yogurt and cheese. If you are looking for weight loss, try skim milk or fat free yogurt.

- Olive oil is the heart of the Mediterranean diet and is used for cooking and dressing.

- Water should be consumed to the recommended 1.5 to 2 liters daily. Herbal infusions and broths are also recommended.

- Wine during meals is part of the Mediterranean diet. Moderation is key. No more than 5 ounces of wine for women or men 65 years and older; men under the age of 65 can have double the recommended amount of wine for women (10 ounces).

- Regular exercise for a minimum of 30 minutes per day.

- Rest and destress where possible. This will do wonders to regulate your body's hormones and revive your soul.

Chapter 2: The Benefits of the Mediterranean Diet

Heart disease, diabetes, high blood pressure and higher levels of cholesterol have seen an increase over the years. This is due to the way the modern Westerner eats and lives. Focusing on a lifestyle laced with stress, limited physical activity, and high in preservatives and processed foods, it's no wonder that many struggle to live a healthy life.

Everything about the Western lifestyle is fast-paced and instant gratification. Have a look at fast foods and processed foods or frozen meals to see what I mean. But, hope is not lost. All that remains is to change eating habits and make lifestyle adjustments. This will include moving away from a highly processed and quick Western diet with limited exercise to a diet rich in plant-based foods, grains and fish, and getting more exercise. This is where the Mediterranean diet can be beneficial to many people over a lengthy period of time.

With cardiovascular disease amongst the leading causes of death in both the US and the UK, it doesn't come as a surprise that the medical health industry has taken on the challenge of bringing healthy living back into the modern home.

What are the benefits of the Mediterranean diet on your health?

Helps lose weight effectively and healthily

The Mediterranean diet is low in sugar, preservatives, GMOs and processed foods, which helps with weight loss, since the body is receiving the right energy it needs to burn. It's easy to maintain and sustain weight loss as well since the reduction in fat and sugar naturally reduces weight.

Nutrient dense and full of antioxidants

When people follow the Mediterranean diet, they provide their bodies with a higher amount of nutrients, minerals and antioxidants thanks to the increased amount of fruits and vegetables consumed, especially when eaten raw.

Improved heart health

The types of fat we consume will either work with our body or against it. In the case of the

Mediterranean diet, which is high in monounsaturated fats and omega-3s, your heart is not facing an increase in unhealthy cholesterol levels. In fact, the opposite happens. By eating a variety of fresh produce, natural fats, and olive oil, your body begins to tackle that high cholesterol slowly bringing it down giving your blood room to flow unhindered around your body. The result, a happy heart.

Prevents and treats diabetes

Since diabetes is linked to an imbalance in insulin levels, the Mediterranean diet is a healthy asset in diabetes prevention and treatment. Why? Because it is a low sugar diet.

Longevity

Because studies show a link between monounsaturated fat and a reduction in cancer, heart disease, inflammatory disease, depression, cognitive decline, etc., you can enjoy a longer life.

De-stress and Relax

Taking time to enjoy your meals with your loved ones, eating the right foods, and having regular exercise, your stress levels are sure to drop while your enjoyment for life increases. Slowing down and physical exercise are vital tools in stress management.

Further benefits including the prevention of:

- Metabolic syndrome
- Stroke
- Alzheimer's and other dementia
- Depression
- Parkinson's disease

Chapter 3 The Mediterranean Diet – Some Fundamentals

Understanding the fundamentals surrounding the Mediterranean diet will empower you and encourage you to stick with this healthy way of eating. There has been much controversy surrounding good fats vs. bad fats, red meat, and olive oil. In this chapter, I want to bring some more clarity to these areas to help you understand how the Mediterranean diet functions and will benefit your health in the long-term. This is a mere introduction, but should be fascinating nonetheless.

Good fats vs. bad fats – how do you choose?

When it comes to weight loss and health benefits, the fats you eat play a vital role. The dominant fat in your diet will either aggravate cardiovascular disease, diabetes, cancer or obesity, or it will assist you in regulating your moods, keep you mentally alert and regulate your weight.

How do you choose the fat that will give you benefits?

Knowing good fat from bad fat is the secret to healthy success. Saturated fat and trans fat fall under the *"bad fat"* category. Saturated fat is usually found in lard, fatty red meats, poultry skin, high fat dairy, and tropical oils such as coconut oil or palm oil. These saturated fats increase LDL (bad cholesterol), which is further aggravated when consumed with refined carbohydrates. Saturated fats increase the risk of cardiovascular disease and type 2 diabetes.

Trans fats are even worse than saturated fats. They are found in margarine, fast foods, fried foods, vegetable shortening, processed snack foods, cookies, cakes, and pastries. These fats don't just raise your LDL cholesterol, they can also suppress HDL (good cholesterol) thus your risk of cardiovascular disease is elevated by three times that of the risk involved in consuming saturated fats.

So what are the good fats?

Your good fats are monounsaturated fats and polyunsaturated fats. These fats can be found in natural produce. Monounsaturated fats are found in nuts, avocados, and vegetable oils, of which olive oil is one.

Polyunsaturated fats are found in seafood, seeds and nuts. The best type of polyunsaturated fat is the omega-3 fatty acids found in salmon, sardines, trout, flaxseeds, or walnuts. Fish are your best source for these fatty acids.

Another fantastic polyunsaturated fat is the omega-6 fatty acids found in tofu, walnuts, seeds, soft margarine, vegetable oils, and so on.

These good fats improve blood cholesterol and reduce the risk of heart disease. Since any form of fat has a high calorie content, moderation should still be used even when consuming good fats.

Let's look at olive oil in more detail, since it is the Mediterranean diet's primary fat.

The role of olive oil

Olive oil has many benefits that have flown under our radar. As the cornerstone of the Mediterranean diet, we should understand the role of olive oil plays in our health.

What is olive oil?

Olive oil is oil pressed from olives. The best olive oil is *extra virgin* olive oil which is naturally extracted and void of any solvents or cheaper oils. Make sure you purchase 100% natural *extra virgin* olive oil to give you the amazing health benefits.

Within olive oil are antioxidants that are known for their anti-inflammatory properties including oleocanthal, an anti-inflammatory that works similar to ibuprofen in its anti-inflammatory effects, and oleuropein, which protects your LDL levels from oxidation. Olive oil is home to vitamins E and K.

Extra virgin olive oil has a higher amount of polyphenols, antioxidant agents that help with inflammation and reduce the effects of aging. These amazing polyphenols work with our microbiome to strengthen our immune system. When consumed with other foods rich in polyphenols the impact on our health is that much better. A **healthy gut** is key to a healthy body and polyphenols help with that.

What are the other health benefits of olive oil? Let's look at them in more detail:

Reduces risk of Type 2 Diabetes

Obesity and metabolic syndrome create a higher risk for developing Type 2 Diabetes.

Studies show that Mediterranean diet rich in olive oil improves blood sugar levels, insulin resistance and blood lipid levels. The result is the prevention of type 2 diabetes.

Potentially prevents strokes

Strokes occur when a blood clot blocks blood flow to the brain often causing brain damage or death to brain cells. **France has been conducting a study** which is part of the *Three-City Study* focused on the vascular risk factors for dementia. Within their study over, 7,625 people 65 years and older from three cities in France participated in this study. Some were given olive oil to use moderately in cooking while others formed a control group and others were encouraged to use olive oil extensively.

After five years, 148 strokes occurred. When analyzed researchers found that those who used olive oil in their diet had a 41 percent lower risk of strokes than those who did not incorporate olive oil in their diet.

Ensures a healthy heart

Olive oil protects the heart by doing the following:

- Protecting LDL cholesterol from oxidation
- Improves the lining of blood vessels
- Helps keep unwanted blood clots at bay
- Reduces blood pressure
- Reduces inflammation

Fights osteoporosis

Osteoporosis occurs when bone mass decreases, causing the bone tissues and bone to become fragile. People with osteoporosis are more susceptible to fractures at the slightest bump.

How we eat impacts the health of our bones. To keep your bones healthy, eat a diet of foods rich in calcium, vitamin D, phosphorus, magnesium, zinc, boron, iron, fluoride, copper. Recommended foods include nuts, seeds, beans, grains, fish, etc. Olive oil has been found to be a good source of calcium, iron, potassium, and sodium.

Another reason to incorporate *extra virgin* olive oil in your diet.

Helps with cancer

Another benefit of olive oil is its ability to protect the skin from the sun's UV rays. It also helps protect your cells against free radicals by neutralizing them. This helps lower both skin cancer and colon cancer.

Research has shown that olive oil assists in improving cell membrane function which also lowers risk of cancer. Olive oil also protects DNA from oxygen damage thus keeping our cells functioning properly and effectively. Research has also identified that oleocanthal helps prevent breast cancer cells from growing while hydroxytyrosol kills colon cancer cells by helping the body block fatty acid synthetase (FAS) activity.

In a nutshell, olive oil helps your body fight off cancer.

For more updated information on olive oil research visit **www.oliveoiltimes.com**

Wine, wine, and more wine

Within the Mediterranean Diet, wine is a fun addition to a meal. Red wine is preferred over white wine for its heart benefits. Red wine seems to have a higher level of antioxidants than white wine. These antioxidants seem to be a large contributor toward a healthy heart although this is not concretely established.

Within red wine are flavonoids, which are high in antioxidants. Flavonoids are found in the grape skin. So if you can't have alcohol in your diet for various reasons, that's ok. You can still receive similar benefits by drinking red grape juice. Flavonoids lower LDL while increasing HDL. They also assist with reducing blood clotting. Flavonoids also help the body resist allergens, viruses and carcinogens.

When it comes to choosing the red wine to go along with your meal, Merlots and red zinfandels may have more flavonoids than white wine, however your dryer red wines are flavonoid rich. Stock up on a few different makes of dry red wines to ensure that you get as many flavonoids and antioxidants with your meal as possible.

Other benefits that red wine seems to bring to its consumers include assisting with weight loss, maintaining good memory, and controlling blood sugar. All thanks to resveratrol – a natural compound in grapes, peanuts, and mulberries and is both an antioxidant and anti-inflammatory.

Wine cautions

For red wine consumption to be healthy, you should stick to the recommended daily intake. Avoid alcohol if you have any of the following:

- Pancreatitis
- High blood pressure
- Liver disease
- Congestive heart failure

When you have that delicious wine with your meal, savor your glass of wine, the food and your loved ones. Allow wine to enhance your meal and social experience. Moderation is key for healthy living.

A word on red meat

Currently, conflict has come into the debate over red meat and its effect on heart health. The Mediterranean diet traditionally tends to restrict red meat consumption to two servings per week while white meat (poultry and fish) have a higher amount of weekly servings.

The current issue is not so much the red meat as it is processed red meats such as deli meats, bacon, and so on. Processed meat or any processed food for that matter is more detrimental to a person's health than natural lean meat.

In this section I am going to list some of the nutrients that your body will receive when you consume lean unprocessed red meat (beef, pork, lamb). Lean red meats have been found to be fairly neutral with regards to their fatty acid profile thus their impact on cholesterol levels is more neutral than previously thought.

Lean red meats provide a variety of important micronutrients including the following:

- Zinc
- Iron
- Selenium
- Potassium
- B-vitamins
- Niacin
- Riboflavin
- Thiamine
- Vitamin B-12

All of these nutrients and more are essential to give your body the best health throughout your life. Children in particular need a moderate supply of iron in their diets to assist their muscular development and amino blocks.

The link with red meat and cardiovascular disease lies in the animal fat which is saturated fat. Thus consuming a fair portion of beef with fat trimmings may give you lovely micronutrients but a lot of saturated fat at the same time. Here's my solution:

As you incorporate the Mediterranean diet into your lifestyle, look for lean cuts of beef. Buy extra lean mince, lean pork chops, and other lean meats such as veal. If you happen to buy red meat with fat on the edges, simply trim the fat off (either before or after cooking, depending on your purpose).

Weight loss

The Mediterranean diet is not about eating multiple plates of pasta and breads. These delicious foods serve as a feature in the overall meal. A side portion of pasta or a slice of bread along with plant-based foods and lean protein. By taking on this mindset, losing weight on the Mediterranean diet becomes more evident.

Can you lose weight on the Mediterranean diet?

Yes, you can. The key is to have long-term weight loss as your goal. This is where fad diets fail so many people. Weight drops rapidly but the moment you stop the fad diet, the weight creeps back on.

By adopting the Mediterranean diet as a **lifestyle,** you will be able to lose the extra kilos and maintain your weight better. The Mediterranean way of eating allows you to eat more food because the foods that you end up eating have a lower calorie intake.

Although you don't need to count calories on the Mediterranean diet, calories play a role in any eating plan. To lose weight, the calories you consume need to be on par or lower than the amount of calories you burn throughout the day. Energy in must equal energy out. If you eat more than you burn, your body turns the excess calories into fat.

Here are a few weight loss tips to implement as you work on your weight:

What's on your plate

Recall your average meal plate. What does it look like? If you are eating more grains, breads, or pastas with each meal, reduce your portion size and increase your fruit and vegetables with each meal. Instead of two slices of bread have one. Cut the pasta in half.

Exercise

Having regular exercise will help your body burn off excess fat while you reduce your portion sizes.

Limit stress

Stress is often the main culprit behind snacking or eating junk food. Work on your time management skills so that you can give yourself at least a good seven hours of sleep and have some time for yourself. Practice stress management skills such as deep breathing, relaxing, and meditating.

Water

Make sure you drink your water. Water helps your body flush out toxins while keeping it well hydrated. Because water is keeping your body working at optimal functionality, you'll feel good about yourself

Good fats

Eating the right fats such as olive oil, avocado, and other healthy fats, you will help your body to naturally suppress your appetite while releasing a slow yet constant amount of energy to your body.

Eat to lose weight

Going long periods without eating will not help you lose weight, instead it will trigger blood sugar spikes. Eat something healthy, even if it's small, every five hours or so. This will help regulate your appetite.

Exercise

Physical exercise goes a long way in reducing stress in your life while releasing a chain of endorphins throughout your body. Where possible, adults should incorporate at least 30 minutes of daily exercise. This could be in the form of a brisk walk, jogging, swimming, or cycling.

Also where possible, include strength training in your exercise regime. Although muscle has a heavier weight than fat, your body will burn fat a lot faster as you develop your muscle mass. Besides this, strength training will help your body support itself correctly, thus taking pressure off bones and other joints. This will go a long way to reducing joint inflammation and osteoporosis, among other things.

Physical exercise will assist your body in regulating weight, burn unwanted fat, increase energy, and give you a better night's rest.

Chapter 4: Getting Started

Now that we have dissected the Mediterranean diet, let's put it all back together and see how we can move from our current eating habits toward a Mediterranean lifestyle. In this chapter, you will find information on how to integrate the Mediterranean diet into your life, what to add to your shopping list, tips for eating out, and ideal portion sizes.

Moving to the Mediterranean diet

In Chapter 1, I listed the daily and weekly portions of food when I elaborated on the Mediterranean diet pyramid. Following this pyramid will help you transition into the Mediterranean diet. Below are a few more tips to help you transition:

- Incorporate more fruits and vegetables into your diet by adding them to your meals and using them as snacks

- Replace refined bread and pasta with whole grains

- Increase your fish intake while reducing your red meat

- Change your dairy from high fat to low fat or skim milk

- Sauté food in olive oil. Olive oil is your dominant fat – try to use it for everything you cook with

- Eat slowly. The slower you eat; the more time you give your body to register that it has food to process in your stomach. This will also reduce acid reflux and indigestion.

- Clean out your kitchen of your unhealthy foods. The reality is, we eat whatever is in the fridge or pantry. Remove temptation by giving your unhealthy foods away to shelters or consuming it before moving onto the Mediterranean diet.

- Start small. Notice what you normally eat and gradually replace it with a healthier option. This can be a gentler way of transitioning your body and mind towards a healthy diet. As the saying goes, *Rome wasn't built in a day*. Take it one step at a time.

- Reduce your salt intake where possible. Salt is known to encourage water retention amongst other things. Cook with salt, avoid adding salt to your food after its cooked.
- Drink water.

Shopping guide

Now that you have begun taking steps towards integrating the Mediterranean diet into your lifestyle, the time has come to go shopping. Stocking your refrigerator and pantry with the right ingredients will go a long way to ensuring your success on this easy diet.

To make things easier for you and because I like to categorize, I've made a shopping list that will cover almost all your cooking needs:

<u>Protein</u>

- Unsalted nuts
- Fish and shellfish
- Beans, peas, and lentils
- Lean meats
- Skinless chicken and poultry where possible

- Poultry
- Eggs

Dairy

All dairy should either be low-fat or fat-free.

- Yogurt
- Sour cream
- Almond milk
- Rice milk
- Hemp milk
- Soy milk
- Cheese (try to find the reduced fat cheeses)

Spices

- Salt
- Pepper
- Cinnamon
- Cumin
- Chili powder
- Cayenne pepper

- Curry powder
- Honey
- Vinegar
- Garlic
- Ginger
- Herbs

Whole grains

- Brown rice
- Quinoa
- Whole grain bread
- Whole wheat pasta
- Whole wheat flour, preferably stone milled
- Whole grain couscous

Vegetables

- Any fresh vegetables. Do try to incorporate a lot of dark leafy greens in your diet since they are full of antioxidants and other nutrients.
- Frozen vegetables

Fruit

- Any fresh fruit that you enjoy. Aim to have seasonal fruits. This will help keep your budget cost-effective while you enjoy fresh produce.
- Frozen fruit

Pantry

- Seeds
- Oatmeal
- Chickpeas
- Black beans
- White beans
- Low-sodium broth

Other necessities

- Dry red wine such as cabernet sauvignon
- Dark chocolate, roughly around the 70% mark
- Unsweetened cocoa

Whenever you see your kitchen running low on an item, write it down on a piece of paper on your fridge or your preferred method of keeping a shopping list. Weekly top up your pantry. Every now and then, take a week or two to cook with the products you still have in your kitchen. This will help ensure that your food always stays relatively fresh and minimizes wastage.

Eating out

Going out for dinner is permitted on most diets and the Mediterranean diet is no different. Making wise choices while out at a restaurant for dinner can go a long way to help you keep the healthy momentum.

Share an appetizer

An appetizer is meant to be a palette tickler. A little bit of food to take the hunger pains away while setting the tone for the remainder of the evening. Order an appetizer that can be shared between you and two other people or order a small platter for the whole table (depending on the size of your table).

Share your main meal

If you and a friend or your partner are ordering the same food, why not share a plate? Sharing a plate of food will regulate the portion size to fit more within the recommended size. Most restaurants tend to provide large plates of food that can easily be split into two meals.

If you don't have someone to share your food with, eat half and request the remaining half be placed in a take away for your next meal.

Say no to fried food

Where you have the option to replace fried food (chips or onion rings) with steamed, raw, or grilled vegetables, seize the opportunity. Request rice or a baked potato instead of chips.

Request your food be grilled not fried where possible. You can also make a specific request that your food be cooked in olive oil and not unhealthy fats.

Choose your drink

Have a cappuccino, tea, seltzer water, glass of wine, or diet soda while eating out.

Dessert

If you want dessert, try to request fresh fruit. If you can't come up with a more "healthy" dessert, share a dessert with the table or hold off until you get home.

Portion sizes

Personally, I have often struggled to get portion sizes right for each meal. At times I have wondered if the recommended portion sizes are too small or too big. Knowing the practical ways to regulate portion sizes goes a long way to removing this ambiguity.

- One serving of fresh fruit = ½ cup
- One serving of raw vegetables = 1 cup
- One serving of cooked vegetables = ½ cup
- One serving of protein = the size of your palm (the base of your fingers to the wrist).
- One serving of bread = 1 slice
- One serving of cooked pasta or brown rice = ½ cup

Chapter 5 Recipes

To help you get started with your Mediterranean lifestyle or to inspire your own creativity, this chapter focuses on Mediterranean recipes. Within this chapter you will find ideas to have easy-to-make meals throughout the course of the day that can be made in the comfort of your home with all the ingredients in a standard home pantry. Bear in mind that this is a limited amount of recipes to point you in the right direction—there are many, many more possibilities.

BREAKFAST

Start your day well with an energy-packed breakfast. These breakfasts will kick your day off on a delicious note while giving your body a variety of healthy nutrients.

Fig Parfait
Preparation: 5 minutes   Serves 1

Ingredients

- ½ cup of granola

- 6 Tbsp. of Greek Yogurt
- 1 Fig
- Honey

Method

In a bowl, layer the granola and yogurt until you have used all the granola and yogurt. Top with sliced fig and drizzle honey for extra sweetness.

Mediterranean Delight Frittata

Preparation: 15 minutes   Serves 4

Ingredients

- 1x onion
- ½ green pepper
- 1 cup mushrooms
- 6 eggs with a dash of skim-milk
- Herbs, salt, and pepper to season
- 1 Tbsp. olive oil

Method

Chop the onion finely and fry in the olive oil until transparent. If you like, you can caramelize the onions. Add the mushrooms and extra olive oil with some salt and pepper. Once the mushrooms are cooked add the green pepper. Cook for a couple of minutes.

In a separate bowl mix the 6 eggs with herbs to season and a dash of milk. Add to the onions, mushrooms, and green pepper. Place a lid on your frying pan and cook for about ten minutes.

Avocado on Toast

Preparation: 10 min   Serves 4

Ingredients

- 8 slices of wholegrain bread
- 1 Avocado
- ¼ cup of feta crumbled
- Olive Oil

Method

Toast the bread either in the toaster or under the grill, depending on your preference.

While the bread is toasting, mash the avocado in a bowl. Add the feta to the mix. Spread your toast with the avocado and feta mix. Drizzle with a dash of olive oil.

Chai Berry Pot

Preparation 20 min　　　Serves 2

https://pixabay.com/en/macro-chia-pudding-coconut-milk-1285670/

Ingredients

- 6 Tbsp. of chai seeds
- ½ Cup of hot water

- 1 Cup of skimmed milk
- Mixed berries (alternatively, any berry of your choice available)
- Handful of chopped walnuts
- Honey as a sweetener (optional)

Method

In a bowl soak the chai seeds in the hot water for fifteen minutes.

Add the skim-milk and honey.

Microwave until hot

Add chopped berries and walnuts.

Whole wheat Pancakes

Preparation 20 min	Serves: 4

Ingredients

- 3 Tbsp. brown sugar
- 3 Tbsp. all-purpose flour
- 4 Tbsp. whole wheat flour
- 3 Tsp baking powder
- Pinch of salt
- 1 Egg
- 1 Cup milk (or more to get that pancake consistency)
- Fried banana and honey as a garnish

Method

Mix all the ingredients in a bowl. Pancake consistency should be a thick yet liquid state.

Place a 1Tbsp of batter for one pancake. My frying pan usually takes four pancakes. You can adjust this according to your personal size preferences.

After 2-3 minutes turn the pancake over. It should have a golden color. Cook on the flip side for another 2-3 minutes or until golden

Take a banana sliced in half (length ways) fry for 3-5 minutes on each side.

Serve hot with fried bananas and a drizzle of honey

Mexican Scramble

Preparation 10min   Serves 2

- ½ Green pepper
- 1 Jalapeno pepper (seeded for less heat)
- 6 eggs and skim-milk
- ½ cup grated cheddar cheese
- 1 Tsp. Olive oil

Method

In a hot pan add olive oil, green pepper and Jalapeno. Fry for 3 minutes.

Add the mixed eggs and skim-milk.

Mix until you have scrambled eggs. Place in an oven dish and top with grated dish. Grill until the cheese has melted.

Serve hot with a slice or two of ciabatta.

Cranberry Oats-o-Delicious

Preparation: 10 min   Serves 4

Ingredients

- 2 cups quick-cooking oatmeal
- 4 cups of water
- ½ cup of cranberries
- ¼ cup chopped almonds
- Cinnamon
- 2 Tbsp. brown sugar

Method

Boil the kettle. Meanwhile, heat up the cranberries, almonds and sugar in a pan. The sugar is to help draw the juice of the cranberries to create a sauce. Cook until your oatmeal is ready.

Place the hot water, cinnamon and oatmeal in a pot. Cook until the oatmeal is ready (about 3-5minutes).

Serve the oatmeal hot topped with cranberries and almonds.

Lunch

Typically, the people in the Mediterranean region have a hearty lunch followed by a two-hour siesta. For a long time, this has been the culture of several Mediterranean countries, however this tradition is rapidly falling to the wayside in the rush of modern life.

While you may not be able to practically have a siesta every day, having an occasional nap or an hour of *"quiet time"* will go a long way to refreshing your emotional and physical well-being. It will also give your body and mind time to rest from the busyness of your week or day.

Now for some hearty yet fresh lunch recipes.

Avo Chicken Salad with Olive Ciabatta

Preparation: 10 min   Serves: 4

Ingredients

- 4 Chicken fillets already cooked and sliced
- 2 whole avocados sliced
- Lettuce
- Basil
- Cherry Tomatoes
- 1 Carrot julienned
- 2 Tbsp. Pomegranate seeds

Method

Wash and dry the lettuce and basil before placing in a salad bowl.

Add tomatoes, carrot, avocados and chicken

Season with some olive oil and lemon juice

For a burst of flavor, add pomegranate (if so desired).

Tuna Pasta Salad

Preparation: 20 min

Serves: 6

Ingredients

- 1 Cup uncooked bow tie pasta
- 2 x 200g tuna tins drained
- 1x shallot
- ½ Cup of green beans
- Lemon zest
- 1 Tbsp. lemon juice
- 3 Tomatoes cut into wedges
- 1 Cup of feta
- 1/3 cup pitted olives halved

Method

Cook the pasta in hot water for 8-10 minutes or until al dente

In a pot cook the beans for 8 minutes so they are cooked but crunchy. Transfer the beans into a pan and sauté them in olive oil for a couple of minutes

Combine the remaining ingredients in a salad bowl and serve your Tuna Pasta Salad with a slice of your favorite whole wheat or health bread.

Chicken Wrap

Preparation: 40 min   Serves: 6 or more

https://pixabay.com/en/vegan-wrap-plant-based-meal-946034/

Ingredients

- 4 Chicken fillets
- 1 Avocado sliced
- Lettuce
- Red cabbage
- Sour cream

- Olive oil
- Roasted carrots

Method

In a roasting pan, coat the chicken fillets with your favorite seasoning. Add some carrots to your pan. Add the olive oil. Cook at 180 degrees Celsius until the chicken is cooked through and the carrots are tender.

For the wrap: Slice the chicken and carrots into strips. Baste the inside of your wrap with sour cream. Place a few pieces of cabbage, carrots, lettuce, avocado and chicken into your wrap. Fold and enjoy

Halibut Sandwich with a dash of lemon

Preparation: 10 min   Serves: 2

Ingredients

- 2 Halibut fillets
- 2 Lettuce leaves
- 2 Tsp Lemon juice
- 1 Tbsp. Olive oil
- 1x Tomato sliced
- 1x Red onion sliced
- 2 Tbsp. Mayonnaise
- 1 Tbsp. Mustard
- Ciabatta or bread rolls

Method

In a hot pan, fry the halibut fillets skin down sprinkled with some salt and pepper for seasoning. After 3 minutes turn the fillet over and cook another 3 minutes. The fish is ready when it flakes apart easily.

Combine the mustard, mayonnaise and lemon together in a separate bowl.

Spread the mayonnaise mixture on your bread. Place the fish on top of the mayonnaise mixture followed by lettuce, tomatoes and onion.

Portobello Mushroom Burger

Preparation: 15 min
　　　Serves: 4

Ingredients

- 8 Portobello mushrooms
- 4 burger rolls
- Lettuce
- 2 Tomatoes sliced
- Cream cheese and chives
- Olive Oil

Method

Cut burger rolls and drizzle with olive oil.

Mix plain cream cheese with some diced chives.

In olive oil and garlic lightly fry the Portobello mushrooms until they are cooked and juicy.

Place lettuce, tomatoes, Portobello mushrooms inside your burger roll.

Enjoy.

Mediterranean Couscous

Preparation: 15 min   Serves: 4

https://pixabay.com/en/couscous-salad-food-lunch-cuisine-933385/

Ingredients

- Basil

- 8 Cherry tomatoes halved
- ½ Cup of feta
- 1x Red onion
- ¾ Cup of couscous
- 1 Cup of chopped cucumber
- Lemon zest

Method

Heat 1 cup of water in a pot. When it is boiling add the couscous and lemon zest. Place a lid on top of the pot to trap in the steam.

Chop the tomatoes, cucumber and onion.

Using a fork, gently lift the couscous and place into a serving dish. Add your tomatoes, cucumber, onion, and feta. Add a touch of lemon zest to garnish.

Nut, mint, and Basmati salad

Preparation: 15 min

Serves: 4

Ingredients

- 1 cup basmati rice
- 2 cups water
- 1 teaspoon spearmint leaves
- ½ cup of mixed nuts chopped (almonds, walnuts, peanuts, or other nuts of your choice)
- 2 Tbsp. Olive Oil
- ½ tsp salt
- 1 Tbsp. of lemon juice

Method

Cook the rice until light and fluffy.

Once cool add mint and nuts.

For a dressing, mix olive oil, salt, and lemon juice and pour over your basmati salad.

Dinner

Dinner is the perfect meal to sit with family and catch up on the days events. Grab a glass of wine, decorate the table with clean, healthy, and tasty food while laughing and talking the night away.

Roast chicken, green beans, and garlic baked potatoes

Preparation: 1 hour

Serves: 4

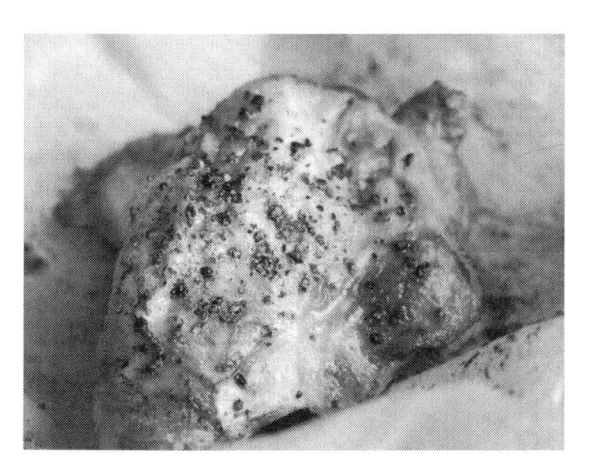

https://pixabay.com/en/chicken-roasted-parchment-pepper-1081088/

Ingredients

- 1x Whole chicken
- 3 Tbsp. Olive oil
- 12 Baby potatoes (or more if needed)
- 2 cups of green beans
- 1 cup chopped tomato

- 1 Tbsp. chopped garlic
- Salt and pepper
- 4 Sprigs of thyme

Method

Heat oven to 200 degrees Celsius. Rub olive oil all over the chicken before adding salt and pepper and thyme. Cook until the chicken has cooked through and the juices run clear.

Boil the baby potatoes until cooked.

Once cooked, add 2 Tbsp. of olive oil and garlic and mix into the baby potatoes

Boil the green beans until tender. In some olive oil pan fry the bean with tomatoes and garlic for 3 minutes.

Serve as a complete dish.

Salmon with Olive and Tomato Salsa

Preparation: 30 min   Serves: 4

Ingredients

- 4 Salmon fillets
- ½ Onion
- 1 Tbsp. lemon juice
- Olive Oil
- 20 Cherry Tomatoes
- 125g of pitted olives sliced in rings

Method

Chop up the onion, tomatoes, olive oil and olives, and combine with lemon juice. Refrigerate for a minimum of fifteen minutes and a maximum of two hours.

In a hot pan place salmon fillet skin down and cook for 3 minutes while basting with the hot olive oil.

Have the oven warm at 180 degrees Celsius. Cook the salmon in the oven for another 8-10 minutes

Serve the salmon hot and topped with salsa.

Lamb chops and couscous

Preparation: Serves: 4

<u>Ingredients</u>

- ¾ cup of couscous
- 8 Lamb chops
- ½ cup chopped tomato
- 1/3 cup chopped cucumber
- 1 Tbsp. olive oil
- ½ Tsp salt
- ¼ Tsp pepper
- 1 Tsp dried oregano
- Lemon zest
- ½ cup of feta

<u>Method</u>

Heat 1 cup of water in a pot. When it is boiling add the couscous and lemon zest. Place a lid on top of the pot to trap in the steam.

Mix olive oil, salt, pepper and oregano to form a rub for the chops. Season the chops with the rub. Grill for 5 minutes or until the chops have reached your preferred readiness.

Mix couscous with tomato, cucumber and feta. Serve with hot lamb chops.

Pasta with Chicken Feta

Preparation: 20 min						Serves: 4

Ingredients

- 1 cup cooked and diced chicken
- 2 cups of penne pasta
- ½ cup of feta
- ½ cup cooked peas
- 1 Tbsp. olive oil and ½ Tbsp. lemon juice

Method

Cook the pasta in hot water until al dente

Drain the pasta and combine with feta, peas and chicken

Dress the pasta with some olive oil and lemon juice.

Baked Salmon with Cheese Jacket Potatoes

Preparation: 40min   Serves: 4

https://pixabay.com/en/salmon-fish-food-dinner-plate-923964/

Ingredients

- Olive Oil
- Lemon
- 4 Salmon fillets
- 16 Cherry tomatoes
- 8 Sprigs of thyme
- 4 Potatoes

- 1 cup Gouda cheese
- Baking paper or aluminum foil

Method

Preheat the oven to 180 degrees Celsius.

Wash the potatoes and cut them in half. Top the halved potatoes with cheese, thyme and pepper. Wrap in aluminum foil and cook for 40 minutes or until cooked through.

Season the salmon with a touch of salt and pepper. Place in aluminum foil together with 4 cherry tomatoes, a slice of lemon, and two sprigs of thyme. Seal the salmon with the foil and cook until the salmon is flaky.

Serve the potatoes and salmon together either in the foil or on a plate.

Sundried Tomato Pesto Salad

Preparation: 12min   Serves: 4

Ingredients

- 2 cups fusilli pasta
- 4 Tbsp. Olive oil
- 1 cup Sun dried tomatoes
- 3 cloves of garlic
- 1/3 cup grated parmesan
- Basil for garnish

Method

Cook the pasta in hot boiling water for 8-10 minutes or until al dente.

Blitz the olive oil, sun dried tomatoes, garlic together until you have a pesto-like paste. Add the parmesan.

Once the pasta is cooked. Mix some of the pesto into the past and top with some grated Parmesan and a few basil leaves to garnish.

Chicken Kebabs and Potato Salad

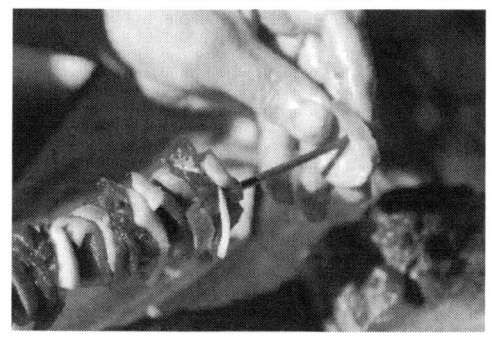

https://pixabay.com/en/barbecue-bbq-beef-chicken-72125/

Ingredients for Chicken Kebabs

- 1x Onion
- 1x Green pepper
- Kebab skewers
- 4 Chicken fillets cut into large cubes

Marinade

- 5Tbsp lemon juice
- Lemon zest
- Salt and pepper

- 3 Tbsp. Olive oil
- 2 tsp garlic

Marinate the chicken overnight.

Method

To make the kebabs, alternate onion, green pepper, and chicken until you have made four kebabs.

Grill until the chicken is cooked through.

Ingredients and Method for Potato Salad

- 8 Potatoes peeled and chopped into cubes
- ½ cup of mayonnaise diluted with skim milk. (I find this helps the mayonnaise coat the potatoes well. Use the milk sparingly)
- 4 hardboiled eggs diced

Cook the potatoes already cubed in a pot of hot water until they are tender yet firm. Drain and cool.

Combine the remaining ingredients in a salad bowl.

Season to taste.

Dessert

Some people love to finish off their dinner with a dessert. With the Mediterranean diet, this is still a possibility; the only difference is that you'd have fruit for dessert more than cake, cookies, and other refined goodies. Here are a few simple recipes, most of which feature delicious fruit.

Figs and Yogo Dip

Preparation: 30min   Serves: 3

Ingredients

- 6 Figs halved
- Honey
- ½ Cup of Yogurt
- Chopped mint

Method

Drizzle the figs with honey. Place in the oven at 180 degrees Celsius to cook until tender.

Mix some honey into the yogurt along with some fresh chopped mint.

Serve figs with a glass of red wine and the yogurt dip.

Fresh Watermelon Salad

Preparation 10min   Serves 4-6

Ingredients

- ¼ Watermelon
- ½ cup of feta
- Mint

Method

Slice up the watermelon into cubes. Mix with feta in a bowl. Add mint to flavor (vary according to your preferred taste).

Serve cold.

Cherry, Prosciutto and Feta Salad

Preparation 20min   Serves 6

Ingredients

- 1 cup of cherries
- 6-8 Slices of Prosciutto
- ½ cup of Feta
- Basil to garnish

Method

Remove the stem and pips of the cherries.

Dice the prosciutto.

In a bowl mix, cherries, prosciutto and feta together. Add some basil as a garnish.

Blueberries, Honey and Yogurt

Preparation: 10 min   Serves 4

https://pixabay.com/en/granola-breakfast-blueberries-787997/

Ingredients

- 1 cup blueberries
- ½ cup of Greek yogurt
- 5 Tbsp. Granola
- Honey for seasoning

Method

Season the apricots with honey. You can either sear them or serve them raw.

Serve with Greek yogurt for a fresh, delicious dessert.

Grilled Peaches and Cream with Granola

Preparation: 20   Serves: 6

Ingredients

- 250ml of cream
- 2 tsp sugar
- 6 Peaches, halved and pitted
- ½ cup of granola

Method

Place the halved peaches in the griddle pan or on the grill. Drizzle a bit of olive oil to help develop a bit of char on the peaches. Cook until tender in the inside and grill marks on the outside.

Mix sugar and cream until white peaks.

Serve the grilled peaches with whipped cream and granola sprinkled on top.

Granola

Preparation: 25 min   Serves 4

https://pixabay.com/en/granola-oats-cinnamon-brown-sugar-683916/

Ingredients

- 7 cups of oats
- 1 cup of honey
- 1 ½ cups of roasted sunflower seeds
- 2 Tbsp. flaxseeds

- 1 cup of desiccated coconut
- ½ cup of oil (your choice)

Method

Preheat the oven to 180 degrees Celsius.

Mix oats, sunflower seeds, flax seeds and desiccated coconut together in a bowl.

In the microwave heat the oil and honey until boiling.

Mix the granola mixture with the honey and oil until everything has been coated. In a tray or oven roasting dish spread the mixture.

Cook for 10 minutes or until a golden color forms on top. Mix the mixture up and cook for another 10 minutes.

Conclusion

Thank you again for reading this book!

I hope this book was able to inspire you toward healthier eating habits while expanding on the benefits of olive oil, red wine, and other aspects of the Mediterranean diet.

This book is a simple introduction to the Mediterranean diet. If you want more information, please continue researching. The hyperlinks within this book will guide you to some further credible sources and studies already conducted. That being said, the internet contains a wealth of information.

I also encourage you to experiment with the recipes adapting them to suit your lifestyle and tastes.

Most importantly, enjoy life with your loved ones. Cherish each moment and spend your life making many happy memories.

If you have enjoyed this book, please be sure to leave a review and a comment to let us know how we are doing so we can continue to bring you quality ebooks.

Thank you and good luck!

PREVIEW OF AQUAPONICS:

Introduction

Aquaponics is a great way to grow fish and food together, but the biggest question for most people is how to grow. Since so many plants do well with aquaponics, it's easy to get over enthused and try and grow everything! With the right set up you can do this but it's also going to be much harder to have healthy plants if you're a beginner so it's a good idea to start out small. Similarly, even if you've picked out plants already growing them in a system that fits your space can be the bigger challenge.

An aquaponic system can be as small as a bucket with fish and a pot fitted on the top, but this is far from efficient. If you're comfortable with the basics of aquaponics, then this is the ideal guide for figuring out the best way to maximize your space and grow all the plants you want to.

The key to having a good aquaponic set up is making sure that your plants get their three main needs met – light, water, and nutrients. Since your water and nutrients are the same thing this means that the grow area has to be adequately saturated or your plants will fail to flourish; too much water, on the other hand, and they may rot. Without having the basics of aquaponic growing down you're already way ahead of yourself. This is meant as an intermediate guide for those already familiar with the basics of how aquaponics works.

When looking for starter plants you'll either want to source those already grown in a hydroponic environment or start them yourself from seeds.

Seed starting in aquaponics really isn't difficult. It's a good idea to start them in a material like coir or rock wool because these are small and will break apart to allow the root system to expand while still providing the support the growing root system needs. It's not advised to transplant plants from a soil environment because there's a huge risk of transplant shock. Similarly, transplanting plants from soil also means you can bring in bacteria and contaminants that may affect your fish. An aquaponic system is a delicate balance which needs to be maintained, both for the health of fish and plants.

To grow your plants well you sometimes have to get a little creative. It's not necessarily about having better equipment but about being smarter with what you have or can get!

What we're going to do is look at a few creative ways to grow your plants and tackle the common problems that plague many growers so that your plants will be the best they can!

Chapter 1 – Creative Growing with Aquaponics

If you're looking to find new ways of growing with aquaponics, then you're probably faced with a problem. While this type of gardening has its own challenges, sometimes we are faced with ones we just can't avoid. The biggest problem that most aquaponics enthusiasts face is space. You'll need enough space to deal with the tank, the grow beds (if you're using them), equipment, storage, access to water and power, and enough light for plants to grow. It's not an easy balance to achieve in the first place but when faced with an environment that isn't conducive to growing plants successfully sometimes you have to get creative.

Space

If your first obstacle is space, then you're going to need to look at growing upwards. This means creating vertical towers or guttering arrangements that are held above your fish tank. Your fish won't be affected by lower light, and it will help you keep the algae bloom down by shading the tank. Your compromise with such a system is that you're going to be limited on the type of plants you can grow. Plants that have large root systems or that require extra stabilization will not work in smaller containers. While this might seem like common sense, you can also look at different varieties as a way around the problem. For example, if you want to grow tomato plants but just can't give up the space for a large grow bed, compromise with a hanging variety that can be grown in guttering instead.

You can also maximize your space by growing your plants strategically. Grow large plants at the back or center of the grow box and grow smaller plants between the others or in front. This will give you the option of growing more plants per box than trying to grow all the same crops at the same time in each. As long as your system is flooding high enough to saturate the grow bed enough to reach all the plants, your only limit is how they are organized and whether you have enough fish to support them.

Light

If you're growing inside or trying to fit a lot of plants together, then lighting can be a problem. To get around this, consider using reflective panels indoors to maximize your light. Reflectors work to bounce any light rays that aren't aimed at your plants back at them. They also reflect heat, so if you're working with a system that needs heating (for example, in winter), then you won't be paying as much for heating by using reflectors. Reflectors can work outside, but because the sun's rays are so strong, they are not advised. A strong reflection can burn plants, melt plastic, and set fire to items, all of which can happen with sun rays when compared to weaker artificial light.

Water/Nutrients

There really isn't a compromise when it comes to the size of your pump. If there's one thing you should opt to go bigger with, it is the pump. The pump is what pushes water and nutrients around your system, and if it's not strong enough you'll find that the plants that are further from the water input may not get watered at all, or in a grow bed environment the water level may not reach the roots. Plants must have water and nutrients, or they will die, there is no compromise. What you can get creative with here is to have two smaller pumps as your system grows and create two smaller systems cycling off a large fish tank. This will also be a cost effective way of growing your system without wasting the pump equipment you already have.

Because your fish provide the nutrition, you also can't compromise on the size of your tank. Without enough fish, plants will not get the nutrients they need to thrive. Too many fish, and the overcrowding can cause disease, death, and fights depending on your variety. You can, however, compromise on your type of fish. Some fish are much larger than others and simply opting for a smaller variety can mean you'll be able to get more fish per tank. This will up your nutrient level in the water. The same can be said for choosing certain varieties of fish over others since they produce greater amounts of waste.

Heat

While most plants will not need extra heating in an indoor environment if you want to grow year-round you'll have to consider heating. Tropical fish species like Tilapia also require heating if you plan on growing year round in a non-tropical climate. To maximize your heat, insulate the fish tank well and consider adding a reflective cover in summer and a black one in winter if you're growing outside. Black absorbs heat while the reflective surface will direct it away on hot days. You can also help maximize your heat by using reflective panels on your lighting if you're indoors. The problem with this is that it's easy to overheat your plants and your fish so you'll also need a ventilation system.

So, the first thing to do when figuring out the best way to grow is to look at what problems you're facing with your space and tackle them accordingly. Let's see a few of the alternative ways you can set up a system to grow plants well.

Check out this book as well!

Printed in Great Britain
by Amazon